Memoirs
of a
Hospice Nurse

ELIZABETH WALTERS

PAGE PUBLISHING, INC.
New York, NY

First originally published by Page Publishing, Inc. 2018

ISBN 978-1-64350-212-0 (Paperback)
ISBN 978-1-64350-213-7 (Digital)

Printed in the United States of America

To the loving memory of all the patients and their families who I have had the privilege of coming into their lives for the past fourteen years.

I have learnt so much from them. My life has been greatly enriched by each one of these individuals that I have met. Working as a hospice nurse has made me a humbler and kinder person. I was forced to be more aware of and to take stock of my own mortality.

Although these patients have all passed away they hold a very special place in my heart. They are gone but never forgotten.

It has been an interesting, exciting, wonderful, and honorable journey as a hospice nurse. One that I would not have changed for anything in the world. Yes, I have loved, learned, laughed, and cried over the years with the patients that I have cared for and their families. Make no mistake, there were many difficulties along this journey. Through it all just observing how these brave men and women faced their mortal challenges toward the end of their lives has been inspiring.

Sincerely,
Liz Walters, LPN.

assess- please note that for LPNs the technical term used for their scope of practice is "observe."

CHAPTER 1

How it began

Growing up as a child, I never dreamt that I would become a nurse not to mention a hospice nurse. I was orphaned two times over by the time I was fifteen years old. My mother passed away in 1974, from lung cancer when I was seven years old. My father succumbed to heart and kidney disease when I was fifteen years old. After the death of my parents, I had to live with my uncle William and his wife, May Rose. However, three years later when I was eighteen years old, May Rose died suddenly and unexpectedly of a massive brain aneurysm.

As I grew older, I experienced other losses of dear ones to me in death. Frankly, I was tired of all the changes and pain that the death and dying caused me. At the age of thirty-three in April 2001, I went to Detroit Michigan to visit a dear older sister-friend, Inez—had just lost her husband, Jim, a few months earlier. Inez and her husband use to live here in New Jersey, and I had become very good friends with her and her family. I met Inez in 1991, and she had become the mother figure that I never had. Inez provided a lot of prudent and motherly advice that I cherished in my heart and valued as a young woman. They moved back to Detroit in 1993, to enjoy retirement. A few years into retirement, Jim was diagnosed with cancer. He fought it bravely for about two years until his death in early 2001.

I had come to Detroit to comfort her in her grief as she had always comforted me whenever I needed it. During my visit with my dear sister-friend, Inez, it was difficult to see the pain that was framed on her face due to the death of her beloved husband of forty-one years. In our conversations, she would often repeat how she had placed Jim in a hospice house in Detroit for the last few months of his life and how the hospice agency nurses took very good care of him. She also added that hospice also provided her and the rest of her immediate family members with guest rooms with amenities for living. This allowed her to stay with Jim around the clock for the final few months of his life until he drew his last breath.

I remember feeling helpless, as I could not heal the wounds that the effect of death had inflicted upon my dear friend. However, I was an active listener that brought her great comfort. I would hold her hands and this always seemed to bring her some measure of peace. Little did I know that this would set the stage for me to embark on a career, where I would be holding the hands of and providing care to people all over the State of New Jersey.

After two weeks in Detroit, the time came for me to bid Inez and her family goodbye and head back to New Jersey. It was a two-hour flight from Detroit Metro airport to Newark Liberty. During my flight back, I started to do some soul searching. I was turning over several thoughts in my head wondering how I could make a positive difference in other people's lives. I was thinking about patients who were approaching the end of their lives and the impact that their passing had on those who they left behind. I knew that I had to do something. I just didn't know what or how to do it.

At this time, I worked for the local area hospital first as a payroll clerk then as a hospital house secretary. I worked the 11:00 p.m. to 7:00 a.m. shift, performing nursing administrative duties for the entire hospital. In short, I was the admissions' personnel for the entire hospital at night. All patients that needed admissions came through me. The night shift always seem to have patients that required ICU/CCU and Telemetry care, so I spent most of my time on these units.

While working on the ICU/CCU units, I witnessed a lot of death and dying up close and personal. Some of these patients had only been on the floor for a few hours. Most were often admitted for MI, CVA, or motor vehicle accidents. I always felt sorry for the patients during their suffering and many challenges that their illnesses would bring. The brave and competent nurses would always do their best to save them and make them as comfortable as possible.

If they didn't make it out of the ICU/CCU, my heart would often break for their family members that would be left to grieve. I was always very sensitive to people's needs. I attribute it to the many losses I had suffered in my own life. I recall feeling so helpless that I was not able to provide the emotional comfort that these families needed. Why? Because my role was behind the desk as a house secretary, *not* a licensed nurse.

As my eyes settled on the flight attendant who was walking down the aisle, suddenly I had an epiphany. The thought came to me, *enroll in nursing school and be a force for good.* This would allow me to not only render clinical care to patients, but I could offer the emotional comfort they and their families needed.

CHAPTER 2

The First Step

In September 2001, I changed my feelings of helplessness by enrolling in the local vocational school for a one-year nursing course to become a licensed practical nurse. I must say, it was quite a difficult task, one of the hardest year of my life. Take it from me, LPN school is no joke. Why didn't I just go straight and become a Registered Nurse? I wanted to get to my goal of making a difference quickly.

I thought I could become a registered nurse while I am helping others as a licensed practical nurse. Not so fast, I soon found out that it is not that easy to make the jump from being an LPN to becoming an RN.

Fifteen years later, I am an LPN who is now pursuing my bachelors of science in nursing degree. "Dare," I say. I have no regrets working as an LPN. My journey as an LPN nurse has been a real learning tree, and might I add a very life changing one. This journey has allowed me to learn, experience, and meet a lot of people along the way that I would, not have met had I gone directly for the RN license. Why don't you read on and see how my journey unfolded unexpectedly.

In order to support myself through nursing school, since I am the sole supporter of myself, I continued to work full-time at the hospital but moved from night shift to day shift and worked on the medical surgical floor as a unit secretary or ward clerk. This is a similar role to a house secretary, but in this role, I was only responsible for admissions for one floor. I am forever grateful to my nurse manager Joan at the hospital. Joan arranged my schedule, so that I could work double shifts every weekend and attend LPN nursing school during the week. Finally, after one year of blood, sweat, and tears, I graduated nursing school in November 2002. I sat and passed the New Jersey State Board of Nursing Exams at my first attempt and obtained my nursing license to practice nursing in February 18, 2003.

My Struggle to Find My Niche in Nursing

Excitement was an understatement to describe my feelings. "I did it!" I screamed, upon learning that I was now a licensed practical nurse. That's right, I could now practice as a nurse.

I was on top of the world, and I was ready to save it from sickness, pain, and grief. I told myself that I was going to be the best hospital nurse there was or so, I thought. However, God had other plans.

My dreams of becoming a hospital nurse was shattered when I soon found out that "nurses eat their young." What do I mean, you ask? Well let me explain. After obtaining my nursing license, I applied to work on the medical surgical floor that I had been working on as a ward clerk. I was told that they did not have an LPN position to offer. A new policy was also in place that LPNs could not work in the ICU/CCU units. I was crushed but wanted to remain loyal to a hospital that I had worked for nine years. I applied to the Orthopedic floor and got accepted. I was in. This is it. I was thrilled and couldn't wait to start taking care of patients. However, it was just not meant to be. I lasted only three months trying to learn from the other experienced nurses who had no patience for me, an inexperienced nurse.

They were too involved in trying to take care of their twelve patients that they were each assigned.

They made it clear to me that they didn't want the added responsibility of mentoring me. God, I felt sick inside. I felt betrayed and abandoned by the very people who had inspired me to become a nurse. You see, these were nurses who I got along with really well while working as a unit secretary and ward clerk. When nursing school got tough, they would often encourage me not to give up.

Yet, once I became a licensed nurse, the relationship changed. It is often said that, "Times change, and people change right along with it." First lesson learned the beginning journey for a new nurse can be a frustrating and lonely one. I am here to encourage all new nurses, never ever give up. If the aspect of nursing you choose initially is not working for you, try another one. One of the many fascinating things about nursing is a nurse has a plethora of specialties to choose from. Eventually you will find your niche.

I started to feel more in the way of my experienced nursing colleagues. I worked the 7:00 p.m. to 7:00 a.m. shift, and as I would drive home, I would often pray and ask God for direction. I had come to realize that I was losing my passion for nursing. I was not feeling fulfilled. I did not like the fast pace that came with working as a hospital nurse.

It allowed me, only a brief moment, to spend with each patient. My nursing colleagues thought that I was too slow and spent too much time with my patients. Coupled with my handicap of trying to hone my nursing skills as a new nurse, I was growing increasingly frustrated. I knew I wanted to give more of myself to my patients.

After only three months of nursing experience, I could see the writing on the wall, and so I made the very painful decision to resign from the hospital. I took a position working in the Dementia unit at a nursing home that was also close to my home.

I enjoyed working with these patients and threw myself into my work. I vowed to do my best and to give all my patients the best nursing care. I soon came to know that each nurse on the floor was responsible for thirty patients, if you worked the evening shift since there were only two nurses that were scheduled on these shifts. If you worked the night shift (11:00 p.m. to 7:00 a.m.), you were the only nurse. Yes, you are right. At night, one nurse is responsible for all sixty patients.

This would include dispensing medications to all sixty patients starting at 5:00 a.m. in the morning. This would also include performing finger stick blood sugars and administering insulin injections if the patient needed it.

I worked the evening shift. Soon though, I started yearning to be able to spend more time with my patients. I wanted to be more of a hands-on nurse instead of just pushing a medication cart down the hallway and dispensing Medications.

Deep down inside of me, I felt a void, but I did not know how to fill it. To be quite honest, I had started to feel that I had made a terrible mistake in becoming a nurse. So in October of 2003, after now what had accumulated to eight months of practicing as a nurse, I was ready to throw in the towel and stop working as an LPN nurse. *Nursing is not for me*, I thought. I no longer felt an inkling of passion for nursing.

I had decided that I would go job hunting and try to get a job as a ward clerk at another hospital. I was disappointed that I had sacrificed and gone to nursing school, and now, I could not fulfill my goal. Then something happened. I call it divine intervention. You see, two weeks before I gave up on nursing toward the end of October 2003, I was working the 3:00 p.m. to 11:00 p.m. shift when a chance meeting with a *per diem* nurse— who was working with me—changed my life forever.

Her name was Eva, and she was also an LPN. During my conversation with Eva, she shared that she was a full-time hospice nurse. *A hospice nurse*, I thought. Surely I had heard and even studied about hospice in nursing school, but I thought it was an RN specialty and not an aspect of nursing for LPNs. I was anxious to learn from Eva. "What do you do as a hospice LPN?" I asked. She explained that she worked for a hospice agency, providing one to one bedside care to terminally ill patients who were exhibiting signs and symptoms of active death and dying. She stated that this level of care in hospice was called continuous care.

Suddenly, a light bulb went off inside my head. I now realized that this was the aspect of nursing that I had been yearning to do. Yes, that was the void that I had always wanted to fill. I gently pressed Eva for more details. I wrote down all the contact information for the hospice agency and decided that I would apply the next day. After I had finished up my shift, given report to the incoming nurse, and bade Eva goodnight, I headed home. Driving home, I was beset with self-doubt and fear. In my mind, I was questioning myself whether I could care for dying patients. I started to reason that being around dying patients would remind me too much of my own painful loss of my parents.

I don't think I ever completely got over my parents' deaths. One thing I know for sure is, we never really heal from the deaths of those we love. I remember the day that death swallowed up my parents as if it was yesterday. I still ache from the loss. There was a part of me that was not sure if I could function in an environment where death and dying was constant.

I turned several thoughts over in my head. I struggled with the thought that I had become a nurse to help, comfort, and nurture people back to health; not make them comfortable to die. I am a strong believer in God, and I always base all my decisions in life around how it will help me to serve him better. So I took my concerns, fears, and doubt to God in prayer. I prayed on it for about two and a half months before I finally made what turned out to be the best decision of my life.

CHAPTER 3

My Journey Begins

I began my career as a continuous care hospice nurse on January 19, 2004, with a—prominent hospice agency in a south central New Jersey suburb. This agency employed the use of LPNs exclusively to render twelve hours or thirteen hours around the clock bedside care to actively dying patients in their private homes or in ALF facilities. Although I maintained a home in South Central New Jersey, the hospice agency required that I traveled throughout all of New Jersey. As a continuous care nurse, I was required to travel throughout the entire state of New Jersey. I covered the northern to the southernmost part of the state and all the areas in between rendering bedside nursing care to many dying patients.

I embarked on this journey as a hospice nurse, not knowing how it would turn out and where it would lead. I must say that after fourteen years of hospice nursing, I have absolutely no regrets. I have faced many obstacles, some social and some personal, during my career. I have come to view them all as stepping-stones on a path that has taught me a lot of powerful lessons that have molded me into the woman I am today.

During my tenure as a continuous care nurse, I have had the privilege of caring for different age groups, ranging from twenty-three years old to one hundred and seven years. They all came from many different walks of life. There were the ultra wealthy, the middle class, and the poor. I cherish and remember them all, but there were some along with their families who just tugged at my heartstring, leaving an indelible mark on my heart.

The first of these dear ones was a twenty-three-year-old named EJ. In the second year of my hospice career in November 2005, I found myself at his bedside. He was the youngest patient to date that I had ever taken care of. Measuring at six feet and one inch tall, with auburn hair, this brave young man was placed on our hospice service with a terminal diagnosis of end stage lung cancer. I found out from his family that he had been battling this rare form of childhood cancer since he was sixteen years old. In spite of his medical challenges, he had put up a brave fight for seven years and had done well for himself. He had obtained a college degree.

Later, he bought a home in the affluent suburb of Montclair, which is situated in North Jersey. He was also in a committed relationship and was enjoying his life.

Then according to his family's accounts in early November 2005, he went in to the famed Sloane and Kettering Cancer hospital in New York City for his regular chemotherapy treatment for his remaining lung. He had been living with only one lung, as the other lung was removed in 1998. It was at this appointment that his oncologist gave him the devastating news: that he only had seven days to live and had recommended that the family place him on hospice services immediately.

On November 15, 2005, and twenty-four hours after what would turn out to be his last visit to Sloane and Kettering, I was dispatched to his bedside by my nursing manager.

My assignment brought me to his parent's home in Oakhurst, New Jersey, an affluent and impressive suburb in the Jersey Shore area. They had brought him to their home so that he could die surrounded by his loving family. As what would become my signature introduction, I would greet all my patients and their families with "Hi my name is Liz, and I am your nurse for tonight." I pulled up to a mansion and was greeted by two lovely people who turned out to be EJ's parents. In addition to his parents, there were three brothers—one older and two younger. In my two years of hospice career, I had learnt to always pay attention to details. I introduced myself to the entire family and was led to EJ's room. I still can picture him. He was lean and frail, but he was well built. Quite a handsome young man, although cancer had ravaged his body. He greeted me with a warm handshake and was equally as gracious as his parents. After we exchanged introductions, I obtained report from the outgoing hospice nurse. I proceeded to carefully assess him and his condition by taking his vital signs to get a base line. Next, I reviewed all his comfort medications and placed them in a safe but easy accessible area so that it would be readily available when I needed to administer it.

In an instant, he bonded with me. I have also learnt that in nursing and especially hospice nursing, it is very important that your patients bond with you. Bonding is important and beneficial for the well-being of both the patient and the nurse.

Some measure of trust is vital in all human relationships no matter the level. Some relationships are on deeper level than others, and so it is with trust.

I had succeeded in overcoming a major obstacle on my first visit. Now I can concentrate on giving him the best care. He quickly opened up to me about his seven-year battle with the rare form of lung cancer that was determined to snatch his young life from him. One thing I observed and admired about this courageous, young man was his ability to remain optimistic in the face of a grave prognosis.

As I cared for him that night, I kept thinking how scared I would be if I was given only seven days to live. To tell the truth, inside, I was terrified; but I did not show it. I was determined to encourage him. After I had got him settled in to bed and gave him his meds to ensure his comfort, I realized that he did not want to go to bed.

He wanted to converse with me. As a continuous care nurse, you are required to stay in the same room with the patient and you must chart on the patient every hour on the hour.

The Continuous Care Nurse must monitor the patient constantly for signs and symptoms of air hunger, pain, bleeding etc. that merit round the clock nursing care and the effectiveness of medications given for each symptom. Which means that the Continuous Care Nurse must be awake at all times.

Sensing that he wanted to talk some more, I gave him my undivided attention. He confided to me that he was afraid of dying because he did not know where he was going, and he did not want to leave his beautiful family. He was also sad that he had so much that he wanted to do and enjoy in life but knew that he would never get the chance to.

I carefully responded that he should take it one day at a time. I then added that if he couldn't do one hour at a time from being too overwhelmed, he should take it one minute at a time. Those words seem to relax and comfort him as I noticed a sense of peace seemed to come over him. Not long after he was sound asleep.

As I watched him sleep, I was praying silently to God to give me wisdom, courage, and the know how to take care of him while bringing comfort to the family. As I have stated before, he was the youngest patient I had ever taken care of, and deep inside, I was scared for him and for myself.

I was having a difficult time with the fact that a young person was going to die and leave his parents and young siblings. There is just something unnatural about parents burying their children. Yet I mustered up courage in my heart after my quiet prayer and calmly conversed with his parents and siblings as they each came in to kiss him good night.

I stepped out of the room briefly to give each family member privacy with him. Once all family members had said good night, I gave his parents an update on his condition. As I searched their faces, I could see that they were still hoping against hope that he would get some more time on earth. I hugged them both. It was my way of showing them that I was on their side. I went back to his room and sat vigil at his bedside to continue my hourly assessment.

As I continued to observe him, I wondered how much time he really had left. "I only have seven days to live." Kept echoing in my head. *What if his oncologist was wrong about this seven-day prognosis that he had given EJ?* I thought. *What if he had a few more months to live?* I had only known EJ and his family for a few hours, but I had felt such empathy and concern for them.

It was now three in the morning, five hours since he was last medicated for pain and shortness of breath. So far, as I observed him, he was resting comfortably without any signs or symptoms of pain or respiratory distress. I was relieved that he was comfortable. The rest of the night was uneventful as he had remained comfortable for the rest of my shift. Prophylactically, I medicated him for pain and shortness of breath half an hour before I gave his morning bath at 6:00 a.m. before the end of the shift. At 7:00 a.m. that morning, I gave report to the incoming day shift continuous care nurse and left him comfortably in her care.

I was barely home at 8:00 a.m. when I received a call from my nurse manager. She wanted to reach out to me before I went off to bed she says. My heart skipped a beat when I saw her number. I thought, *did he have a sudden change in condition in the short time I left him and pass away?* I reasoned she was calling to give me a new assignment. At that moment in time, a wave of sadness settled over me because I did not get a chance to say goodbye to him. It turned out my flight of thoughts were all wrong.

In fact, my nurse manager was calling to tell me that EJ and his parents had called up and asked to speak with my nurse manager. They wanted to request that I would be assigned every night to his case for the next six days, or the end of his life, or whichever came first. If they could not have me as his nurse, they would switch to another hospice company. I was touched, what can I say? I am deeply involved in my faith and usually never miss my Thursday evening Bible study. However, I felt in my heart that God wanted to use me to help this family so I gladly agreed.

Second Night

Night two started out quiet and peaceful. I got report from the outgoing hospice nurse. I did my routine assessment on EJ, answered all questions and concerns of his family, and sat down at his bedside to do my charting. Suddenly, a young man walked in I had never seen before. He came and knelt by EJ's bedside, held his hands and gently kissed him on the head. I had started to leave the room to give them privacy when EJ asked me to stay. He introduced me to the handsome young man with sleek black hair. He had striking Mediterranean features. I found out that he was of Italian heritage and was the love of EJ's life. I greeted him and with EJ's permission, gave him a brief update on his condition.

After his significant other left the room, EJ looked at me and asked, "Do you still view me the same?"

"What do you mean?" I asked.

To which he responded with a full question, "Will you see and treat me differently now that you know that I am in a same sex relationship."

I quickly reassured him that as a nurse, my job is to take good care of my patients and not to judge him, his lifestyle or family. I saw his body relax as a smile danced over his face, and a wave of peace settled over him. I knew based on his body language that he was relieved to hear me say this, and most importantly, that he believed and trusted me as his nurse. That made me feel fulfilled. I never would want any of my patients to feel that their personal life or the way they choose to live would be cause for me to judge them.

As night two wore on EJ would occasionally exhibit signs and symptoms of shortness of breath or air hunger. Oxygen was applied at the dose that the physician ordered, and we had our nightly chat that he would always end with the words "thank you for being here for me, and thank you for listening." EJ, by all accounts, was comfortable on this second night under hospice care. He had only needed morphine for shortness of breath, only once during the night. He was receiving Dilaudid IV, continuously via a PCA pump for pain. So far, he had only needed to press the bolus button on his PCA pump to give himself a rescue dose for break through pain once.

As day broke for the next day and as is customary, I gave him medication for pain shortly before I gave him his bath. Day three had now arrived, and my shift was almost over. He started to cry. As I knelt by his bedside to provide emotional support, he looked at me and stated, "Oh Liz, I only have four more days to live." You are trained to remain strong and professional for your patients and not breakdown, but I could not help welling up with tears.

Nonetheless, I held his hands, looked into his eyes, and spoke gently to him. I validated his feelings of fear of death and dying and of the unknown. I reminded him that although difficult, he should continue to take life one day at a time.

I reported off as usual to the incoming nurse and asked her to have our hospice social worker follow up with EJ and family during the day for psychosocial support.

As I drove home, I was besieged by anxiety. You see, like EJ, I too was subconsciously counting down the days to his impending death. I wondered if he would pass on my shift. He had told me this particular morning through tears, that was his wish. Whenever I am troubled, I usually turn to the one who loves me the most, God, for help. So as I drove home that morning through tears, I poured out my heart to God. Imploring him for guidance, wisdom, and help. I had come to realize that this was turning out to be one of my toughest cases.

Nights three, four, five, and six were pretty much routine, and I was glad to see that his spirit was up. His significant other never left his side. Although, the features of grief and sadness were imprinted upon his face. He was very supportive of EJ. The parents and siblings also were doing their best to stay strong for EJ.

The morning of day seven came, and EJ was still alive. "This is nothing short of a miracle his family exclaimed. Maybe EJ's oncologist was wrong," they reasoned. I was cautiously optimistic and could not help to show my support for him. He was so happy that he was still alive on the very day his Oncologist had predicted that he would die. Another lesson learned: Medical personnel cannot actually predict the exact day that someone will die.

The irony of the situation is that on day seven, EJ actually appeared to look and feel better. He attributed it to my kindness and good nursing care. I humbly accepted his compliment and told him that I saw it as a privilege to be his nurse; and that, it was the care and kindness from the entire hospice team including the other shift nurses, social workers, and chaplains.

On this morning as I drove home, I felt a sense of relief. It had seemed as if EJ had proved his oncologist's prediction to be wrong after all. Maybe he will be around for quite some time. That morning I slept well for the first time in seven days.

CHAPTER 4

Night Seven

At 7:00 pm, I was back again to pull my twelve hour shift with EJ. Day seven had come and was almost over. I was happy to see him sitting on the side of his bed dangling his feet on the floor when I arrived. Physically, he still looked as if he was getting "better." Oddly enough though, I could sense that he was emotionally down. He greeted me warmly as always and gave me his usual thumbs up. Then before I could say you are welcome, he thanked me for taking such good care of him for the past six nights. He now turned and looked at me sadly and hit me with this statement, "Oh, Liz, you are such a good nurse, too bad I am never going to see you again since I am going to die tonight."

I was floored. I regained my composure and responded with this question. "EJ you are comfortable so far aren't you?"

He replied, "Yes," and echoed once again, "but I am going to die tonight."

He also started to ask about his grandmother who had passed away only a few days earlier. The family had asked that her death be kept a secret from him so as not to cause him any additional pain, since he was especially close to his grandmother. He then said that he was no longer afraid to die because he was going to be with his grandmother.

To be honest with you at that time, I was still a relatively new hospice nurse and didn't know what to make of his sudden change in emotional state. I listened actively and provided as much emotional support that I could. I also notified his parents and my on call Triage RN Nurse as per protocol. Soon, he summoned each of his family members including his life partner to his bedside. He wanted each to come in individually so that he could say his good byes. He also requested that I stayed in the room as he tearfully bid goodbye to his loved ones.

His goodbyes to his parents and life partner were emotionally hard for all involved. I supported them the best way that I could. All of this took place before twelve midnight.

I tucked him in to bed at 9:00 p.m. that night after giving him his comfort meds. I checked his PCA pump, and it read that he had enough Dilaudid to last him for another forty-eight hours. He was also maintained on fifteen liters of oxygen. He was observed to be comfortable at 9:00 p.m. and had denied having any pain or short-ness of breath. Soon he was sound asleep and noted to be resting comfortably.

Day Eight at Twelve Midnight

At exactly twelve midnight, without warning, EJ woke up out of his sleep gasping for air and complaining that he could not breathe. I quickly administered the as needed dose (PRN) of morphine that was prescribed for shortness of breath. I also placed him in the High Fowler's position to help facilitate his breathing.

Nothing I tried worked. I could hear his lungs filling up with fluid without using my stethoscope. Yes, the unthinkable was hap-pening. EJ was actively dying. I calmly pressed the button in his room to signal to the family to come to his bedside.

He realized that he was actually dying and demanded in a weak voice that his father, his partner, and I get him out of the bed so that he could stand up. He wanted nothing to do with his bed. It was as if he wanted to run away from death. He started to exhibit signs and symptoms of one of the classic symptoms of death and dying called terminal restlessness. I gave him Ativan, which is the drug of choice, often used in hospice for terminal restlessness; but it was not effec-tive, and he raged on. As per protocol, if Ativan does not work and the patient is displaying extreme restlessness then the nurse has to move up to the next drug of choice, Haloperidol. I administered one milligram, I remembered under his tongue and hoped and prayed that it would work. I was so scared inside, but I had to remain professional and strong for EJ and his family. I also reached out to my on call triage nurse to send out the on call RN for support for the family and of course, me.

After getting a verbal order to increase Haloperidol to two milligrams every four hours as needed from our on call medical director for his restlessness, EJ calmed down a bit but still insisted that we assist him out of bed. Well, don't ask how his father, his partner, and I did it, but we got him out of bed so he could stand up. All three of us supported his now limp-six-foot-and-one inch frame while he started to cry bitterly that he didn't want to die. Then he turned, looked at me, and cried out, "Liz, please don't make me die, help me to live again. I just don't want to die. How do I say goodbye to this beautiful family I have here?"

Well, there was not a dry eye in the room. I felt as if my heart was being ripped out of my chest. I heard myself feebly reply, "EJ, don't you know that I can't give you life, but you know who can? God and he is going to take care of you."

You see, I had done everything as a nurse for him. As instructed by physician, I had given him the increased dose of Morphine for shortness of breath, Ativan and Haloperidol for terminal restlessness respectively, increased his oxygen to the maximum allowed by tank to twenty liters per minute. Yet he was fighting so hard that the body could not relax so that he could pass away peacefully. It is that will to live that kept him fighting. I have come to know that the younger the patient is, the harder they fight to live. Who can blame them? Who wants to die? No sane person I know.

I felt helpless as I stood there trying to help his father and partner support him. It was at this critical time when in my heart I said a quick prayer and prayed to God for peace and for help. Suddenly, I found myself stroking his face and uttering the following words, "EJ, be at peace. God knows how to take care of you."

Without warning, after he heard those words, the fight was over. We felt when he went limp in our hands and just like that I noticed that he was no longer breathing. No, there was no rise and fall of the chest wall.

A hush fell over the room, and the three of us gently placed him back into his bed. I then allowed the family to say their final goodbyes to him and grieve their loss. I offered emotional support to the family including his partner. Our on call RN nurse arrived a few minutes after his death to pronounce him. In the state of New Jersey, an RN has to pronounce a patient in the home, assisted living facility or nursing home. I provided post mortem care after. I stayed with the family until they gave me permission to call the funeral director that they had made prior arrangements with.

Through it all, I never left the family. I waited with them until the funeral directors came and helped them take EJ into their care. I walked behind the gurney that took him to the hearse that would take him to the funeral home. Walking out with him was moment of closure for me. I returned inside and spent another few hours with his family. Despite their loss and grief, they all told me how they were glad that he had passed away at night so that it could be on my shift. They couldn't thank me enough, and again, I reassured them that I had done it with all my heart in it.

I must say, as I drove home at 5:00 a.m. that morning, I had mixed emotions. I was relieved that he was finally at peace, but I wished that his death hadn't been such a fight. The picture of him begging me not to let him die kept tugging at my heartstrings. I took two weeks break from work after EJ's death. I wanted to do some soul searching since I was having second thoughts about continuing to work as a hospice nurse. During that two-week hiatus, I discovered that this was part of my DNA as it were. Comforting and taking care of the most vulnerable. After all, that is why I chose to become a nurse in the first place. I decided that hospice is where I belong, and I would continue the journey.

CHAPTER 5

The Journey Continues

I am glad I didn't quit halfway on my journey in hospice. Had I done so I would not have met and been given the opportunity to meet these other precious souls that later invited me into their lives. When I returned to work, my next assignment took me to the home of a precious twenty-nine year old girl by the name of DC. She lived in the southern town of New Jersey by the name of Forked River.

DC was stricken with end stage cervical cancer. I remember vividly that it was two days before thanksgiving Day. She was laying down in her bedroom, and she too had a loving mother and father. After assessing her and making sure that she was comfortable, the bonding process began with us getting to know each other through conversation. Her mom was present in the home, and both her and DC tearfully related that two years prior, DC started to see signs that alerted her to go to her local clinic for a checkup.

Although she had a job and was working, the job did not offer its employees health insurance. In the year 2005, the laws were different then, and employers were not bound by law to offer insurance. She was over twenty-one years old so her parents couldn't carry her on their insurance. That left this precious young woman without health insurance coverage. She had gone to the clinic to see the doctor because she did not have to pay to see him. However, when she saw the clinic doctor after his examination, he told her that she needed to see a specialist—an oncologist to be exact. She also needed to have a battery of lab testing to rule out cervical cancer.

I often think of her because she is one patient that did not have to end up with end stage cervical cancer. It is well known that cervical cancer once detected early is one that the patient is most likely to recover from. For DC, things didn't turn out that way as she and her mom continue to relate. After her visit to the clinic's doctor, she tried desperately to find a job that offered her health insurance since she was from a humble, middle class American family of modest means and could not pay for oncologist visits and lab and cat scan procedures. Eight months later, after her clinic visit, she found one. Three months later, she was legible to get health insurance from this new company.

It had been eleven months later since she was advised to see an oncologist. However, when she finally saw him, the news was devastating. She had stage four cervical cancer. Her loving family did not want to give up, or accept that there was nothing else that could be done. This had been such a crushing blow to her parents. They decided to help DC fight by seeking aggressive chemotherapy and going through trial programs at Sloane Memorial hospital. When that didn't work, they enrolled her in holistic programs. Unfortunately, the cancer was relentless, and her oncologist gave her six months or less to live.

I really found this quite troubling. Life and good health are our two greatest assets. Bearing this in mind, I am a firm believer that all humans in America should have good health insurance. I was deeply hurt that because of not having health insurance, a twenty-nine-year-old woman who had her whole life ahead of her would be soon cut down in death due to a delay in getting care.

I did my best to provide emotional support to mother and daughter. She was still able to walk and really did not look as if she was terminally ill, if she did not share it with you. Once I had given her pain medication, she was quite comfortable. I remember that night when I first met her, she shared that she loved beautiful lingerie. She had two draws filled with them. That night before she went off to sleep, she seemed to not believe that she was going to die. I say, this because she was talking about things she had planned to do when she started to feel better.

She had a good night. Her pain was managed throughout the night with the medications that I had given her. She slept all night, and that morning when I offered to help her with a bath at 7:00 a.m., she told me that she preferred to take showers and did not want to take her shower until later that morning. After giving report to the incoming hospice nurse, I bid her and her mother goodbye with the understanding that I would be back that night.

I came home that morning and quickly fell asleep. I woke up at 5:00 p.m. that evening, and when I checked my messages, one was from my nurse manager, informing me that DC had passed away suddenly earlier on in the day. That was shocking. No one including me thought that she would pass away so soon. We all thought that she had a few more months at least to live.

I thought of her family. It was thanksgiving day eve. I notice that death always seem to come knocking around the holidays that occur at the end of the year. I tried to find out from my nurse manager what happened that caused her to die suddenly. She related that our medical director thought that she had a pulmonary embolism. I never got to say goodbye to her or to hold her hands as she died, but I often think of her and how her young life was cut short because of lack of health insurance. She is one of the reasons why all humans should have solid and good health insurance. We can't put a price on life now can we? DC will be forever in my heart. Gone but not forgotten.

CHAPTER 6

Another Journey

After my experience with DC, on December 5, 2005, I moved on and went to work for another reputable hospice in North Central, New Jersey. Since my change to this new hospice agency, I continued to care for several other people who hold a special place in my heart.

Four years later, in 2009, I was given an assignment in the town of Woodbridge in North Jersey. I was sent to care for a thirty-year-old young man named PB. He was a photographer with National Geographic Society and was based in France. He had done well for himself and had recently sent for his girlfriend in America to come to France. Once she arrived in France, he had only proposed to her about six months prior, and they had planned on getting married in the near future when the unthinkable happens.

When I arrived at his home in Woodbridge summer of 2009, I was greeted by his tearful parents, fiancée, brother, and other extended family members. I received PB in bed unresponsive to words and touch. He was breathing, but I noted that his breathing was labored. He was jaundiced from head to toe. I was the first nurse to start caring for him which means that I was opening the case for continuous care. I did my evaluation and assessment on him and quickly gave him Morphine for his labored breathing. I also applied oxygen to him according to the physician's order. He still did not awaken but after fifteen minutes he was breathing easier and was noted to be much more comfortable.

His father chose to entertain and sit with the rest of the family members in the living room. His mom and fiancée, who both were equally distraught, chose to stay with me at his bedside. His mom continued to tell me the story that she had started when I first walked through their door that evening.

PB and his girlfriend's life changed forever shortly after they got engaged. How so? Well his mom stated that PB started having severe itching and just started to not feeling well. He took some time off from his assignment and went to a few different doctors who could not seem to find out what was wrong with him. Soon, he and his girlfriend noticed that his skin was yellowing and returned to the physicians, yet they could not find anything wrong. His fiancée stated that she was not sure if it was the language barrier that prevented the doctors in France from diagnosing him. Each day, he grew weaker and his fiancée realized that something was seriously wrong. It was at this point that they both decided to reach out to his parents in the States.

His parents went to France to see him, and when they saw him, they made the decision that PB needed to be back in the United States very quickly. PB, his fiancée, and his parents flew back to America, two days later. Once back on United States soil, they took him immediately to a reputable hospital in the union county area. He was admitted to the hospital with diagnosis of end stage liver cancer. Yes, those four words would change PB's life and future. He was discharged home from the hospital earlier on that morning to home. His attending physician had written an order for him to go home on hospice care immediately.

His fiancée reported how devastated she was, and how she saw all their dreams, plans, and future together disappear once they found out he was terminally ill. She was only twenty-five years old and was a widow as it were before they even tied the knot. She was devastated. She was from Atlanta, Georgia, and had reached out to her family for support. She had been staying with PB at his parent's house for the past two weeks.

I have found out that it is very hard to comfort people especially when matters of the heart are involved. Nonetheless, I prayed silently and did my best to comfort his fiancée. It was clear to me that all of this was surreal to her. As the night wore on and as I continued to monitor PB's condition from my observation, I realized that he was not going to be long for this world. He was actively dying. He was not uncomfortable as I had been monitoring his breathing and had medicated him when necessary. He remained unresponsive, but there was no sign and symptom of pain noted. His face was relaxed, and he was not moaning.

Eventually, his mom retired to bed, but his fiancée remained with me at the bedside. I could tell that something was weighing on her mind. I decided that I would let her reveal it on her own if she chose to. Finally, she started to become tearful. I placed my arms around her and asked her what was wrong. I advised her that we should step away from the bedside. Another lesson learnt in hospice is that although a patient may be unresponsive or unconscious, the hearing is always the last thing to go. I did not want to discuss anything troubling close to his bedside. So we moved away from his bedside but remained in the room.

His fiancée revealed softly that she had been contemplating going home to her parents and forgetting this tragic chapter in her life. The sudden and unexpected change in her life's circumstances in such a short time had taken its toll on her. She was torn and emotional about handling his impending death. She had planned to pack her two suitcases and seek refuge in her parents' arms the next day. She just could not stand to watch her young fiancé, PB, as he lay dying. She had not mentioned this to his family because she did not want to hurt their feelings.

A flood of thoughts was floating around in my head. I was trying to process quickly what I had just heard. I am no expert in counseling, but I decided to speak with her from a place of love and kindness. I asked her how he would feel if she bailed on him now. She hung her head, and at that point stated that if she was the one stricken with cancer, he would never have left her side. I was glad to hear her say that. With this been said, I encouraged her to stay until the end. That somewhere down the road, God would reward her for her loyalty. I validated her feelings of fear, panic, and sheer disappointment but also helped her to see that loyalty was important. I helped her to see that his parents and other family members would be devastated; and of course, if PB woke up and found that she had deserted him when he was at his lowest point, that would be heart breaking. I could see that the veil of sadness had lifted from her face. I am not sure though how much I had reached her heart, but I thanked God that I was able to give a listening ear to this young woman.

Soon after, she decided to retire to bed. I was left with PB and, of course, my private thoughts. PB remained comfortable, and I only needed to continue to monitor his breathing and to manage any signs or symptoms of pain or terminal restlessness. I gave him oral care and had changed his sanitary brief, and now he was clean and dry.

As I sat back down to chart my nurse's notes, I started to think that it had been five years now since I had been practicing as a hospice nurse. I had met so many patients and their families, each with their own unique family dynamics. I had vowed in my heart that regardless of the issues each family that I meet would face, whenever I had the privilege to care for their loved one, I would always try to be positive and be a source of encouragement for all.

It was 7:00 a.m. the next morning, and PB had made it through the night, but he remained unresponsive. I gave him a warm bed bath and turned and repositioned him for added comfort. In my heart, I had harbored the thought that I would not need to come back that night. I did not think he was going to make it through the day. As I waited for my relief nurse, I could not help feeling a bit sad inside. He was one of a handful of patients that I had rendered care to when they were already unconscious. In essence, he will never get a chance to meet me. I always go the extra mile for these patients. There is something so heartwarming and fulfilling when you take care of someone who will never know that you were ever at their bedside.

My relief nurse came, and I gave her a detailed report. I gently whispered in his ear, "goodbye," although I knew that he could not respond, but I knew that he could hear me. I said goodbye to his family as well and let them know I would be back that night if PB was still with us.

I went home and went off to sleep quickly. I kept waking up and checking my phone messages. I was so sure that I would get a call from my nursing office informing me that he had passed away. Yet that call never came, so I reported to work at 7:00 p.m. that night. What a surprise when the out-going nurse informed me that PB was awake. In fact, she said he had been awake since twelve noon that day. I was anxious to meet his soul. Although he was awake, he remained nonverbal and was only able to nod and shake his head in response to a question. Yet I was so glad that I could look into his eyes and tell him that I was there to care for him throughout the night.

I remember him smiling at me and nodding in approval. As is protocol in nursing, I performed a head to toe assessment on him. Straight away, I noticed that he was mottled from his feet up to his thigh. Mottling is decreased blood perfusion. Skin may become mottled and discolored. Mottling and cyanosis of the upper extremities appear to indicate impending death. When mottling of the skin of the knees, feet, and hands starts, death often occurs within twenty-four hours.

One of the challenges of being a bedside-continuous-care nurse is that I have to update and prepare the families for their change in status and impending death, so I gave him his nightly bath and medicated him for pain and shortness of breath. Even though he was unable to tell me that he was hurting, I could see him grimacing in the face, and that signified to me that he was in pain. I gave him all medications for pain and about twenty minutes later, he fell asleep and was very comfortable. I seized this opportunity to update the family of my findings during my assessment. I gently broke the news to them that his circulation was shutting down. Even though he was awake, and alert death would probably occur within twenty-four hours. I wanted to prepare them mentally and emotionally for what was to come. As I sat down with his parents and fiancée, my goal was to give them a chance to grieve even before they lose their beloved PB. I allowed each family member to honestly state the emotions they were feeling. I provided the listening ear and gave them emotional support. His family showed incredible strength in the face of adversity. They all stated that they had come to accept that he would pass soon. I was glad that the family was in a "good place" or as good a place that they could be in given the circumstance.

One of the many lessons I have learnt in hospice is that everyone grieves differently. Some members will continue to show a strong front while others will be withdrawn or show anger. This family portrayed a strong front. When a dying patient sees that their loved one is at peace, it makes it easier for them to pass away and not linger. Incidentally, it seems that PB had sensed that his family was ready to let go because I could see that he was not struggling as he entered the final phase of the death and dying process. No evidence of terminal restlessness was observed instead he seemed to have lapsed back into a comatose state. As the night wore on at 3:00 a.m. that morning, he passed away peacefully with his family at his bedside.

The usual protocol was followed, which involves allowing each family member to pay their final respects, and the hospice registered nurse being dispatched to pronounce him. After pronouncement, and after I had rendered post mortem care, I waited with the family for the arrival of the funeral directors. The family used this opportunity to thank me for the two nights though brief that I had come into their lives and made a difference. To my shock and surprise, his mom chimed in and said that she wanted me to know that she had overheard the conversation the night before that I had with PB's fiancée during which I encouraged her to remain with him until the end and not cut out on him. She revealed that when she heard me utter the words admonishing the fiancée to be loyal, it was what brought her to a place of peace. I was humbled and honored when she told me this.

For a certainty, I have come to know that your words have power and can affect others positively or negatively. Lesson learned, always make sure that your words are positive and up building. One never knows the impact your words will have on people. It is an experience like this that made me soldier on and continue to serve others at the bedside. Soon, the funeral Directors arrived, and after making sure that the family was in an area that they could not see him been taken into their care, I assisted them with getting him unto the gurney. I also took my last walk with him as they took him out to the vehicle that was going to take him away. I am the kind of person that needs to continue until the end. Making that routine, last trek with patients that I have cared for makes me feel that I have seen them through until the end.

I spent another hour with his family just to make sure that they were holding up well. I am sure they will grieve as the days wear on, but I always like to make sure that when I leave the family members after a death attendance that I leave them relatively at peace. Driving home this night, I thought about what he would have become had he not been cut down in death. It is often said that cemeteries are the richest places on earth. How so? Because in all cemeteries are buried several dreams, aspirations, great doctors, nurses, lawyers, and photographers, like PB, and the list goes on and on.

CHAPTER 7

Guiding a Precious, Young Mother through Her Final Journey

As my journey continues in 2009, it took me to the doorstep of a young thirty-five-year-old mother of two and wife in Hillsborough, New Jersey—a town in the western suburban part of the state. She had two very young children. A boy aged six, and a girl aged three. Her husband was as you would imagine close in age to her too. Her name was LT. When I arrived that evening to take care of LT for the first time, she was not at all conscious.

Unfortunately, she had entered that phase where she was already actively dying. After I had gone through the normal routine of getting report from the outgoing nurse, meeting with the family, I went in to assess LT. She was a beautiful lady. She was stricken with cancer of the sinuses. Yes, that is right. You can get cancer in your sinuses. Her husband told that for over a year, she started having issues with her sinuses, and her physicians had attributed her sickness to sinus infection.

After a year of misdiagnosis, it was finally discovered two months ago that she had a rare form of end stage cancer of the sinuses. This left her and her family with little time to prepare to say goodbye to her young family. As I administered her medications and gave her a warm bath, I was moved with pity for her young children, especially her three-year-old daughter. This felt like déjà vu to me. I started reflecting on my own mother's sickness and ultimate death. Only difference is, I was seven years old. It was difficult for me to process then so how do you explain death to a three-and six-year-old.

After I made sure that she was comfortable, I sat down with her husband and her concerned parents and in-laws. The children were distracted with cousins who were closer to their age who played with them. It was all agreed that the children will need grief counseling during and after the loss of their beloved mother. I reassured the family that I would reach out to our bereavement coordinator to set up a bereavement program for the family and, especially, the children. My company's policy is that our social workers and bereavement coordinator call and visit family members of patients who were on our service for up to thirteen months.

In between monitoring her condition as the night wore on, I did my best to support her family emotionally. She was comfortable and just lay there with her eyes closed. Occasionally, I would hear her moan, and sometimes, I could see that she was having trouble breathing. I medicated her to keep these symptoms under control. As her young children played until it was their bedtime, they seemed protected by the gift of being an innocent child having a child's mind. Another lesson learned is that, as adults, sometimes it is good to see things the way a child does that is not worry about things. I have found this to be a protection when I am faced with adversity.

She made it through my twelve-hour shift, and her husband and the extended family would take turns checking in on her. They all appeared to be coping appropriately with her impending death. I admired her husband's courage. He had done everything he could to maintain a normal life for his children. That morning at seven, I gave her another warm morning bath. I applied aromatherapy to her chest, arms, and legs. In hospice, aromatherapy is often used as a holistic method to help the patient's body to relax. Aromatherapy is used only after the patient's skin is tested, at least twenty-four hours prior to applying it to the skin.

When I left her in the care of the incoming hospice nurse, she was comfortable. I could see that she was travelling, but I did not know if I was going to need to come back that night. I kissed her goodbye and whispered in her ears for her to take care, and that, it was my privilege to have taken care of her. I also added, "God will take care of your children." I gave her husband an update on her condition then left since I had already given report to the incoming nurse.

Although I had left her comfortable, my heart was heavy. I am very sensitive to other people's needs, and I could not help thinking about her two young children. I went home and followed through with my promise to reach out to the bereavement coordinator to arrange for our social workers to visit the children.

I went to bed shortly after. I woke up at 4:00 p.m. that evening to a message from my nurse manager informing me that she had passed away at 2:00 p.m. during the day. I was bombarded by a flood of emotions. I am so glad that I whispered those last words in her ears. Although I never get to see or hear from her family again, every year that comes around, I think that her children are one year older. Her daughter will be twelve-years-old and her son will be fifteen years old now. I always hope that they are all doing well. Yes, LT, a precious young mother, gone too soon, but never forgotten.

CHAPTER 8

A Bitter Family Feud that Hinders a Young Father from Crossing the Creek

As the year 2009 continued, my Journey brought me next to the doorstep of SM, a thirty three year-old male stricken with glioblastoma. This is a fast growing malignant tumor affecting the brain or the spine. Symptoms usually involve severe headaches, vomiting, and seizures. SM, my patient, had been experiencing these symptoms for a year, his wife relates. I remember this continuous care case as if it were yesterday. I was off that weekend, or so I thought. It was a Saturday afternoon, and I was home relaxing when I received a call from the triage nurse requesting that I help-out with a continuous care case for both Saturday and Sunday.

This young man I found out, when I arrived, had a very prestigious job on wall street in New York City. He lived with his wife and two children in a sleepy bedroom community in South Central, New Jersey called Hazlet. SM and his wife, FM, were both originally from Ireland, and they both had a lovely and thick Irish Brogue.

His wife was only two years younger than him. They had got married in Ireland when they were in their early twenties, then headed to America to make a life for themselves. The union produced two precious children, a son who was only five years old, and a daughter only two years old. She tearfully reported that he had been having headaches on and off again for about a year now. He would often take the train in to New York for his job on Wall Street, but the headaches got so bad, that she was soon driving him in to the city after she had put the children on the school bus.

She told that she kept encouraging him to go see a doctor so it could be checked-out, but he did not like to go to doctors. Then one day, one year and three months ago, as she drove him to work, he had a big seizure accompanied by uncontrolled vomiting. This forced them to turn around and head straight to the emergency room at the local hospital near their home. That day, as FM reports, was the start of their fifteen-month battle against glioblastoma. She went on to relate that SM was admitted that day that he had his first seizure on the neurological ICU unit at the hospital, and after several tests, they were given the news that no young family should ever have to hear. SM had stage four glioblastoma and only had fifteen months to two years to live.

It was exactly fifteen months since SM had been diagnosed, and now upon arrival to his home this Saturday evening, I found him in bed moaning aloud on and off and trashing around violently. I had to politely listen to his wife as she gave me his history while I worked quickly to get him comfortable. I have learnt over the years that all cancers in the end stage can be painful; however, any form of brain cancer is one of the most painful cancers one can endure. Tumors in the brain are rarely painful on their own, largely because the brain itself has no pain receptor, but they can press up against the blood vessels or nerves that surround the brain and steadily build up pressure. This pressure can lead to significant discomfort.

After I had carefully and quickly reviewed SM's comfort medications that were in the home, I administered Morphine for pain and Ativan for anxiety and terminal restlessness respectively. When he continued to trash around in bed and rattle his bedside rails, I had to go to the next drug of choice for terminal restlessness that is Haloperidol for extreme anxiety.

For some people, when Ativan is not effective, Haldol is usually used to sedate a patient displaying psychotic behavior. He was unfortunately displaying psychotic behavior. Even after he had received the Ativan, he was still trying to rip out the rails on the side of his bed.

Finally, twenty minutes after receiving the Haldol, he calmed down; and the trashing around in bed stopped, and soon, he was noted to be sound asleep. The loud moaning had stopped too. I straightened out his wrinkled bed sheets that had taken a beating during his violent trashing. I took care not to wake him up. According to the family, he had been moaning and restless since about ten that morning. His primary physician and neurologist had recommended hospice. The family, especially his parents, who had flown in from Ireland a week ago, was very resistant to hospice. They had told his wife loud and clear that they wanted SM to continue to fight. The decision to choose hospice or not to choose hospice turned into a family feud. His parents were very angry at their daughter in-law, for placing him on hospice. They accused her of trying to kill him.

As I entered the home that evening at four in the afternoon, the tension was palpable. My company had asked that I open the case three hours earlier. His parents, two brothers, and two sisters—who had also come in from Ireland along with their parents—were barely on speaking terms with his wife. They blamed her, wrongly accusing her that she did not seek medical attention sooner for him. She felt as if she was under constant attack from his parents since her family had not yet come in from Ireland, and she was all alone. She also had the two young children to care for and shield from their father's suffering.

I must admit, it was a very tense atmosphere to be in, and I was only there for a few hours and was presented with multiple crisis with SM being so ill that I had to focus on him first. I did not get to bond with him because he was too restless. I had to sedate him, and once he was comfortable, he had quickly fallen asleep.

Now that he was asleep, everyone in the home, myself included, wanted him to get his much-needed rest. What can a hospice nurse do?

Although I had only met his wife for a short time, I could tell that she was a dedicated wife and mother. His family was not accepting of his terminal illness and was clearly looking for someone to blame for this tragedy. To her credit, however, she kept on being

45

polite, kind, and strong for her beloved husband and of course her children. As he rested quietly, the bad blood and feelings within the family continued to rear their ugly head. It was difficult to watch his older parents and adult sisters and brothers take turn at throwing out insults at his wife and at another female in-law—who was originally from Scotland and was visiting to give them moral support. I knew that his parents and siblings were under severe stress and were completely devastated, but their behavior did not give them the right or excuse for the way they were treating these two women.

It was one of the most uncomfortable situations I had ever found myself in. I did quietly reach out to our triage nurse and asked her to have the social worker and chaplain on call visit this family. I felt that this family needed to have some form of spiritual and emotional healing within themselves, if not they would implode. As they continued their tirade against the two grief stricken women, especially his wife, I could see that he was waking up and had started to become restless again.

Medical tests and theories have proven that the hearing is the last thing to go when humans are actively dying. This had proven true with SM because, although he could not make his needs known, he could still hear and sense that there was tension around him.

I had to spring into action and medicate him for terminal restlessness and pain issues again to ensure his comfort. Within half an hour later, he fell asleep again but I could hear him groaning in his sleep. It was the hardest thing to hear. That groaning was not physical pain but more emotional pain. It was as if his literal heart, mind, body, and soul were crying out. I tell you, needless to say I was very upset about this. I felt that he was hurting deep inside because of how his wife was been treated. He could not be at peace so he could pass peacefully because he was worried about the turmoil he was leaving behind. This is called unfinished business.

This needed to be resolved so that his mind, body, heart, and soul could relax and be at peace in order for him to make his transition. It was 6:00 p.m., and soon, there was a knock at the door; and I was relieved when I saw our hospice social worker and chaplain standing there. I had reached out to our triage on call nurse earlier for backup emotional and spiritual support, not only for the patient and family but for my own emotional and mental support too. Another important lesson that I have learnt as a nurse is always seek help from your colleagues when you feel that you need it. Do not be ashamed or feel that you should go it alone. Every aspect of nursing requires team effort from all disciplines. That is even more the case when you are in hospice nursing since the nurse is giving so much of herself.

I led the way for my two colleagues down the hallway of their home to the living room, where his parents and siblings were camped out drinking Irish coffee, eating pastries and commiserating. My two colleagues were given a full report of the family dynamics prior to their arrival by our triage nurse. So after I had introduced them to each family member including his wife, I took my leave to continue to give him my undivided attention. Silently, in my heart I prayed for peace and healing for this family. Without being judgmental, this family— I could tell—needed a spiritual healing. I was hoping that the chaplain and the social worker would help them to come to that place where they realized, that now more than ever, they really are going to need each other.

They needed to have love and mutual respect, which I had noticed was so lacking. His wife was loving, kind, and respectful; but her in-laws, not so much. As I returned to his room, I was relieved that he was still sound asleep.

Occasionally, I could still hear that faint groaning in the spirit. I decided to apply aromatherapy to his chest— especially, on the left side where the heart is located—his hands, legs, and back to help his body and mind to relax. The results were with good effects. The low spiritual groaning went away as he continued to rest.

Two hours later, the hospice SW and chaplain emerged from the living room. I could see that they too, like me, were trying to hide how they felt about this family. I could read their faces that they thought this was going to be a challenging case to say the least. My patient, by all accounts, was a kindhearted, calm, and respectful person before he was stricken with Glioblastoma. His wife was humble and kind. Yet his parents and siblings were so different.

Sadness and grief can make good and ordinary people act in strange ways and can bring out the worst in them. It would not have been wise for these two ladies to discuss their feelings, or for me to voice my concerns openly or to state how I felt while we were in the home. The goal is always that the hospice team ensures that there is little or no stress for most important the patient, who is nearing the end of their journey and, of course, the families.

Bearing this in mind, they both tapped me on the shoulder and told me that some important issues were involved, and that they would each send me report later that night in an email. All disciplines were given a Blackberry at that time (remember those), so we could communicate while out in the field with each other and with our cooperate office. They were going to fill me in as it were.

I went to the living room and saw that at least they were now speaking with his wife. I used the excuse that I wanted to give them an update on him that he was very comfortable and was not in pain. It is true that I wanted to provide them with the good news that he was at least comfortable and not in pain. However, I wanted to search their faces and try to see what emotions and feelings they held.

They seemed to be pondering over the discussion that they had just had with the chaplain and social worker. It seemed as if the rest of the night would be peaceful.

The emailed report did come in later that evening from both the social worker and the Chaplain. They gave me all the details of the conversation, which helped me to understand the root of his family's bitterness and hostility towards his wife. In a nutshell, the feud was all about money and inheritance. He had made a lot of money from working on Wall Street, and the family wanted to make sure that they would get some of it. Apparently, when he realized that his disease was terminal, he had made a will so that the wife and their two children would be provided for after he was gone. It did not surprise me that families fight over money, what surprised me was that his parents and siblings would choose to do it at this delicate time.

As a nursing professional, though armed with certain knowledge of different family dynamics, you have to remain neutral and focused. The patient, entrusted to your care, is your main priority; and their emotional and physical wellbeing is of tantamount importance. The report I received from social worker and chaplain also provided a ray of hope and reassurance that they believed that the relationship between wife and family would improve albeit temporary.

They had educated the family that a feud could hold a dying loved one from passing away peacefully. This is because they find it hard to leave a loved one who they feel may not be able to cope with their death, or who may be in some form of trouble or danger. This worry about their loved ones usually cause the dying person to linger. This brought some comfort to me, and I felt better about being in the home.

I continued to care for him throughout the night. He would occasionally wake up moan on and off, but this time, the moan was a physical moan. It was 10:00 p.m. at night, the house was quiet, and the usual hourly loud noise and bickering among the family was finally absent. His loving wife had brought the children in to kiss their semi-conscious father goodnight before she tucked them in to bed. I was especially touched when she placed her toddler daughter in the bed with him briefly. She instinctively placed her face over the left side of his chest over his heart and started kissing her father all over. He, in response to the love and tactile stimuli from his baby girl, tried to lift both of his weak dying hands to hold her. One thing I have come to know for sure is that love is a powerful emotion, and it conquers all things, even the powerful enemy death.

Shortly after that, he fell into a deep sleep. It was 11:00 pm, and his face looked so relaxed, not tight. I had given him all his medication, and he was very comfortable. I continued my vigil at the bedside as his family retired to bed. It was 5:00 a.m. that Sunday morning, I had to bring the family to the bedside as he made his transition. They all held hands and formed a circle around his bed as he took his last breath. Once he had passed, they hugged and cried on each family member's shoulder. They decided that they would not wake the children to tell them their father had passed away. They would tell them later in the morning when they woke up.

After the usual and normal steps were taken—that is post mortem care, pronouncement, and finally handing him over to the care of the Funeral Directors and my usual last walk out with the funeral directors—I bid the family goodbye. I left the home at 8:00 a.m. that morning. I could only hope and pray that this family was going to come together for the good of the two youngest family members, the children. I was relieved that he was able to finally go peacefully, once he no longer had to hear his family quarreling in the background. I saw it as a privilege that I was there to help his precious wife and the two young children in their time of need. I am truly grateful to the hospice social worker and chaplain who came out to support me and to help the family to come to a place of peace. The expression "no man is an island" certainly is true, especially for hospice professionals.

CHAPTER 9

Saving a Live-In Caregiver from Doing the Unthinkable

It was only a week later after I had cared for my patient in Hazlet that I found myself back in the township of Hazlet. This time, I was charged with taking care of a ninety-year-old lady who was in the home alone with a live in caregiver who was originally from the Philippines. I never know fully what I am walking into as I visit these homes, but I never entered a home or an assisted living facility without first praying and asking God for guidance. As a nurse, you always get report, but I have found that every home has a different spirit or feel and, of course, different dynamics. I always wanted to be protected spiritually before I started my work. This is what has kept me safe and sane no doubt in this line of work.

So when I pulled up at this humble home this Monday evening, I had no idea what was about to unfold that night. The report that I had received from my nurse manager, since I was once again opening the case, was the patient had no living family members. Her lawyer, who was acting as her power of attorney, lived in another town in New Jersey. He had, however, hired a caregiver to live in her home and take care of her around the clock. When I arrived, I met the small petite caregiver who told me that she was originally from the Philippines. After inquiring how my patient was doing, I got a lengthy report from the caregiver.

Soon I went in to meet my patient so that I could access and start taking care of her. This patient was in no position to speak. She was at the very end of end stage Alzheimer's type disease process. This was evident by her inability to hold her head up, respond to verbal stimuli, and her confusion. She was severely contracted, and her legs were touching her abdomen. In spite of this, I still introduced myself as I would to someone who was not cognitively impaired. I gently stroked her hair and hands in my attempt to bond with her. You see I wanted her to feel safe through my touch. One thing I have found out is that sometimes a patient stricken with Alzheimer's sometimes have brief and rare moments of lucidness. I made sure during my assessment that she would be pain free and, of course, comfortable. I then gave her a warm bath, turned, and repositioned her on her side for comfort. As I placed her tiny teddy bear in bed with her that I had pulled out of her Essence of the Journey bag that I had brought for her, I could see a little smile dancing on her face. You see, one of the things that sets my hospice agency apart from the rest is that we have specialized hospice programs. One such program is the Essence of the Journey Program. This is a specialized hospice program for our patients with late-stage or advanced dementia with a strong emphasis on education, assessment, and multi-sensory interventions. Our mission is to deliver a personalized approach of comprehensive hospice care and services with integrity and compassion.

Our goal is simple: to honor and respect the individual as they prepare for their final journey by providing an individualized plan of care, specific to their dementia needs.

Our approach involves multisensory interventions designed to engage the core of the person and promote interaction by incorporating all of the senses: sight, sound, smell, taste, and touch.

A special care package is designed with each patient and family member in mind. Each customized care package contains supplies to encourage care of the mind, body, and spirit to promote quality of life.

This particular bag that I brought had a teddy bear and, of course, a clean blanket. I also placed the blanket on her too. Although she could not speak, I knew I had made an impact on her. She was still in there, and I knew it. I went through the normal protocol while tucking her in, to make sure that she had all her comfort medications. I did all my safety checks making sure that her oxygen, bed, and all her necessary equipment were in place. Once she was safe and comfortable, I turned my attention to her live in caregiver who had helped me wash, clean, and turn and reposition her.

It is so important to have a good relationship with the live in caregiver in a home. As I sat down to converse with the caregiver, I could tell that something was troubling her. I was eager to get to the bottom of what was troubling her because I did not want anything to interfere or affect the care that my patient would receive.

Still, I was not prepared for what I was about to hear. She soon revealed that she was a single mother with a twenty-year-old son who was away at college.

She went on to explain that she lived in South Jersey, a good two hours away from Hazlet. As mentioned before, she was a very petite woman who looked about sixty years old. She was very soft spoken, but I soon found out that she was a woman who was deeply troubled and who was planning on doing the unthinkable.

I am not sure why she chose to unload her burdens on me, but I must tell you, I am glad she did. She related that after a series of bad breaks and the financial meltdown of 2008, she had lost most of her money save for only sixty thousand dollars that she had left in her 401K account. She was very depressed about this because she had to pay college tuition for her son. He was her only child. All they had were each other. They had family in the Philippines, but they were not close. She was barely scraping by financially, although she was working so hard. She wanted to provide for her son since he had a promising future. He was studying to become an engineer.

She felt that her life was over, and there was nothing to live for. The last straw she told me came about two months ago when her dentures fell into the toilet bowl, and now she has to go without teeth, which made her feel that she was less attractive. She was not going to replace these dentures. No, you really cannot make this stuff up, yet I was delicate with my response. I am sensitive to people's needs, and I know that a woman of any age is always concerned about her appearance. I made sure to validate her feelings letting her know that I understood how she felt being a woman myself. I gently and softly told her that she had her son to live for. She agreed with me on this, and then, she dropped this bombshell:

She revealed that she had planned her own murder. "What did you say I asked?" Thinking that I had heard wrong. She repeated it again that she had carefully mapped out a plan to get herself murdered. I could feel my insides churning, but I was determined to learn more. I did not want to come off as judgmental for fear that she would shut down on me. I decided to play along with her to try to get as much information as I could. I did not know how I could help her, but I was hoping that I could talk her down from it as it were.

She then told me that she had lost most of her life's savings and really had nothing to live for. She wanted to make sure that when she was gone her only child, her son, would be well provided for. She further went on to state that she was going to buy a lot of fake gold jewelry, such as necklace, bracelets, and earrings. She was going to get all dressed up in her Sunday best and put on all her jewelry. She chose the city of Camden in New Jersey as the place of choice where she was going to loiter about at a well known spot, where she was sure that she would be robbed and murdered. Unfortunately, the city of Camden is often ranked as one of the deadliest cities in America and regularly has the highest violent crime rate in the state.

I needed time to digest all of this. To say this story and plan was unsettling, is an understatement. She spoke about her well-laid and diabolic plans with such calmness and peace. I could see that she was resolute in what she had planned to do. Although the story was unnerving, I mustered up courage and asked her how getting murdered would benefit her only child. Her response provided the motive. She had taken out life insurance on herself that would offer a big payout to her son should she die sudden and unexpectedly.

I continued to speak with her calmly without making her feel that I was in any way judging her. As I tried to reason with her, I found myself saying at one point, "What if they do not do it right. What if it is a botched robbery and you are only maimed and not killed then what?" The situation could prove to be much worse than she could ever imagine, not only for her but her beloved son. I noticed when I said that it appeared as if she was meditating on what I had just told her, yet she stated that she needed to leave her son in a good place financially.

I realized that she was depressed. It is often said that you should speak consolingly to the depressed souls and try to comfort them. I wanted her to give my patient good quality care as her live in caregiver. Silently in my heart, I wondered how would she continue to care for my precious patient with her state of mind. Quite frankly at this point, I do not know who I was more worried about, my hospice patient or the live in caregiver. I knew I had to try to change her way of thinking and her mind set. I did not know how to start. I was there to work for this patient who needed my care, and now it seems that I had a full-blown crisis on my hands that had nothing to do with hospice care which was why I was there in the first place.

I concluded that if I helped her, I would ultimately have helped my patient. I always bring a small pocket Bible with me. I-Pads were not as popular then as it is now, and I was not tech savvy. I decided to share a comforting scripture with her. I asked her if it would be all right for me to do so, and she agreed. I shared Philippians chapter 4 verses 6 and 7. There, it encourages all human beings not to be anxious about anything but to take everything to God in prayer, and God's peace will safeguard our minds and hearts and give us peace. I actually had her read these words from the Bible, and as she read these words, I could see that life was coming back to her eyes. I then shared another scripture with her, and this time, it was first Peter chapter 5 verses 6–8. This Bible passage admonishes people to cast their cares on God because he cares for us.

This Bible passage really struck a chord with her. She read the same verse that stated "because he referring to God cares for you" at least four times. She then looked at me and started to cry.

"I needed to hear those words," she said. For so long she stated, "I have felt like God has abandoned me, and so, I have been feeling hopeless and depressed."

I encouraged her that we all face difficulties, but one thing all humans can do that is free and cost nothing is to pray to the highest force in the universe who cares for us. He really does, and he really knows how to help each and every individual. I did not want to sound preachy. I only wanted to save this lady from herself. I genuinely cared for her well-being.

Throughout that night, as I monitored and cared for my precious patient, I encouraged the live in caregiver to continue to draw close to God. She told me that she was going to be going home the next day, as another aide was coming to relieve her since she had been working on this case for the past seven days; and it is the policy of her agency to give the caregiver a break after being on a case for a week. I was wondering if I had reached her heart. Without being too preachy, I told her that God would never let her down. She only needed to seek him out as a friend. I placed a Bible based journal and my small Bible that I had in my bag with her. I wished her well. Really that is all I could do.

The next morning came, and after reporting off to my relief nurse, I said goodbye to my patient and, of course, to the caregiver. I gave her a hug, and again told her that I would be praying for her. I could not stop thinking about her on my ride home. I was not sure if I was able to convince her not to carry out her sinister plan and harm herself and ultimately her son. I really hoped in my heart that I was able to change her mind.

I had taken a few day days off from work and was not going back to work until the weekend. Actually, I was not scheduled to go back until that Saturday. I rested up for the rest of the week. It was now Friday morning, and I had just woken up. It was about 9:00 a.m. when my home phone rang. It was the live in caregiver, who I had talked out of killing herself on the other line. I had stepped out of my normal character and had given her my home phone number that night when she poured her heart out to me and had told her to call me if she felt that she just needed someone to talk to.

The voice on the other end of the line greeted me with words of someone with a new zest for life. She had called to tell me that she had pondered over our conversation on Monday night, had read over the Bible and Bible-based booklet I had given her; and she had called to tell me what an impact this had on her. She shared how all the encouraging words and scriptures that I shared with her had given her a new lease on life. Her mind and heart now felt light, she said. She had called to thank me because she had decided to abandon her plans in staging her own murder. She had decided that there was more to live for, and it was not worth it to take her life. I tell you, this is no joke. I really could not believe what I was hearing. I do not take credit for this. I believe that I was just the instrument that God used to save her life.

I have learnt that God brings people together for a reason. I told her how happy I was for her and encouraged her to stay strong. I have never heard from her again; and I have not heard of her death so I trust and hope that wherever she is, all is well with her mind, body, and soul. I never did get to go back to care for the patient in Hazlet that Saturday because, soon, the call came in later that Friday during the day that she had passed away peacefully at her home. Another lesson learned is, do not be afraid to be a friend, even to a stranger. You never know you may be saving a life.

CHAPTER 10

Facing My Own Mortality When I Almost Came to the End of My Journey

On Friday, December 30, 2011, I reported to work for my usual 7:00 p.m. shift. I had not been feeling well for the past week. I was experiencing extreme weakness and tiredness. I had to force myself out of bed.

This evening, I was scheduled to provide continuous care nursing to the father of one of our medical directors. This was an eighty-year-old Filipino gentleman who was stricken with cancer. I headed to his home in Old Bridge, which is in Middlesex County—another town in the central part of the state.

The moment I walked into his room, I realized that he was in pain. His wife and extended members of the family were all present. Our outgoing nurse was also present too. After she reported off to me, I worked really hard to get him comfortable that night. The cancer had reduced him to a mere eighty pounds, and he was drifting in and out of consciousness. The outgoing nurse had done very well in keeping him medicated with Morphine for his pain issues, but it had started to wear off; so once I took over, I made sure that he was comfortable.

It was a lot of mental pressure on me since all the family was at the bedside crying on and off and displaying anxiety about his condition. Coupled with that, I was just not feeling well, I did not know why, but I was having a tightness in my chest.

Nonetheless, I was determined to put my best foot forward. I never led on to how sick I really felt. I remember just kept praying in my heart that I would be able to go home early that night. My patient did not appear that he was going to make it through the night; and so I thought well, if he passed in the early morning hours, at least I would be able to go home and rest, just rest I thought.

I have to say that I am glad that this was one of my prayers that God did not answer. Had he answered that prayer I would not be here today. You see, after I had struggled through the entire night with my feelings of general malaise, weakness, and lethargy—that morning Saturday, December 31, 2011, shortly after giving report to my relief nurse— I collapsed on the floor suddenly. It was reported that I had briefly fainted.

My colleague, with quick thinking, placed me in a recliner geri chair that was in the room and reclined it and elevated my feet so that blood would go to my heart. She then alerted the family members. I am a no-drama person, and I really did not want the family members to see me like this. I was truly embarrassed. They were however a very loving and kindhearted family. Our medical director was present in the home as well. His wife was also a medical doctor. She was just as lovely and compassionate to me as the rest of the family. Immediately our medical director decided to call 911 to get me to the nearest hospital. I was weak but still alert and able to make my needs known. So I made two requests: I asked if I could go to CentraState hospital which was much closer to my home, and I also asked if I could avoid going in an ambulance. Unheard of you may say. I am just a very low-key person that just does not like a lot of attention and fan fair as it were. He lovingly instructed his wife to drive me to the hospital using my car while another family member drove behind us so that she could take her back home.

We arrived at the ER, and she went inside with me and told them about my collapsing and my symptoms. She stayed with me until I was given an observation bed in the ER. Tears brimmed up in my eyes when she hugged me and wished me well. I did not know it at the time, but my life was forever going to change. The ER nurse drew a slew of stat blood work from me. I felt that for each blood draw, I was getting weaker and weaker. An hour later, the ER doctor came and informed me that my blood count a.k.a hemoglobin was only 4.6, and I was actually in a very precarious position. I was actually bleeding out internally from a ruptured fibroid, and if I did not get a blood transfusion, I would actually die.

I do not think I mentioned it before, but I will now. I am one of Jehovah's Witnesses and have been since 1990. Although I love and cherish life, I know that blood is life. I hold firm in my belief that I will be obedient to God's command in the bible at Acts Chapter 15:28–29 where there humans are admonished not to take in blood. Both the Old and New Testaments clearly command us to abstain from blood.

Jehovah's Witnesses seek the best possible medical care for ourselves and our families. When we have health problems, we go to doctors who have skill in providing medical and surgical care without blood. We appreciate advancements that have been made in the medical field. In fact, bloodless treatments developed to help witness patients are now being used to benefit all in the community. In many countries, any patient can now choose to avoid blood-transfusion risks, such as blood-borne diseases, immune-system reactions, and human errors.

At one time, the medical community generally viewed strategies for avoiding transfusions, so-called bloodless medicine— as extreme, even suicidal, but this has changed in recent years. For example, in 2004, an article published in a medical education journal stated that "many of the techniques developed for use in Jehovah's Witness patients will become standard practice in years to come." An article in the journal *Heart, Lung and Circulation* said in 2010, that "'bloodless surgery should not be limited to Jehovah's Witnesses but should form an integral part of everyday surgical practice."

Thousands of doctors worldwide now use blood-conservation techniques to perform complex surgeries without transfusions. Such alternatives to blood transfusions are used even in developing countries and are requested by many patients who are not Jehovah's Witnesses.

With these facts in mind, I soon found myself locked in a life and death struggle with the CentraState hospital's clinical team when they offered to start blood transfusions on me, which I refused. I did; however, being a woman of sound mind, advise hospital personnel that I would take the following blood fractions listed below based on these facts:

Blood fractions. Fractions are derived from the four primary blood components—red cells, white cells, platelets, and plasma. For example, red cells contain the protein hemoglobin. Products developed from human or animal hemoglobin have been used to treat patients who have acute anemia or massive blood loss.

Plasma—which is 90 percent water—carries scores of hormones, inorganic salts, enzymes, and nutrients, including minerals and sugar. Plasma also carries clotting factors, antibodies to fight disease, and such proteins as albumin. If someone is exposed to a certain disease, doctors might prescribe injections of gamma globulin extracted from the plasma of people who already had immunity. White blood cells may be a source of interferons and interleukins, used to treat some viral infections and cancers.

Should Christians accept therapies incorporating blood fractions? The Bible does not give specific details, so each one must make his own conscientious decision before God. Some would refuse all fractions, reasoning that God's Law to Israel required that blood removed from a creature be poured "out on the ground" (Deuteronomy 12:22-24). Others, while refusing transfusions of whole blood or its major components, might accept treatments involving a fraction. They may reason that at some point fractions that have been extracted from blood cease to represent the life of the creature from which the blood was taken.

In my weakened state, I laid out all these facts to them, but they were upset and viewed me as a religious fanatic who was going to die and was willing to throw my life away at forty-four years old. I must say I was scared to die. Once I refused blood transfusion, they basically ignored me. They kept passing me on the gurney. I reached out to my congregation elders and asked them to come quickly which they did at record time once they heard that I was hospitalized.

As each hour passed, I was getting weaker and weaker. I had arrived in the ER from 8:00 a.m. that morning, and it was now 1:00 p.m., and I was still in the observation area in the ER and still on the gurney. They said they were going to admit me, but no one was doing anything. The Elders in my congregation arrived and tried to advocate for me, and most importantly, they tried to have me moved to Englewood hospital in Englewood—where they are known worldwide as one of the few hospitals in the United States and in the world whose medical personnel know how to treat and build up patient's blood count without the use of blood transfusion.

Unfortunately, hospital personnel would not authorize my transfer citing that my condition was too delicate and unstable for me to travel in an ambulance. I was still awake and alert, and I knew that if I did not get help soon, I was going to die. I did not like how I was made to feel because I refused blood. I did not reveal that I was a nurse, but I could not help feeling betrayed all over again by these people.

I finally was transferred to a room with a bed to a med-surg floor that evening at 5:00 p.m. They may as well had left me down in the ER or better yet transfer me to Englewood hospital where at least I would be treated. The nurse hung a bag of iron IV solution and did not bother to hang a bag of saline solution. Oh, my God, receiving that iron without the normal saline burned so much. I told her to stop running it.

Things were not going well, and I was depressed. My blood count had since dropped to 4.2; and I was afraid that sooner or later, I was going to lose consciousness, and I was going to lose my life. I was flooded with a ton of emotions. I was being ignored, ostracized, and not cared for properly because I had taken a stance for obeying my heavenly Father. All the years of my practicing nursing, I never made a patient feel less than. I always endeavor to make each person that I cared for feel that they were the most important person on the planet. I always honored and respected their wishes and their beliefs.

It also has never mattered to me what the color of their skin was. All humans are entitled to good care.

That Saturday, as I lay in my hospital bed, I did not sleep. This sickness had come down on me so suddenly that I hardly had time to call my family. My family is rather small and are in New York, so most of my support came from my brothers and sisters from the congregation that I attended. I knew that some would be visiting the next day, Sunday, since they had started calling once they knew that I had been admitted on the floor. One thing I knew for sure was that I wanted to be out of this hospital. I wanted to be transferred to Englewood hospital. Funny when you are the patient. You always feel so helpless. I wanted to live, and this was a matter I prayed about all night long to Jehovah God. It seemed as if my life was slipping away.

Sunday morning arrived, and I was still alive even though my blood count was dropping. As the morning progressed, and as the afternoon rolled around just as I expected, some of the elders/pastors from my congregation came to visit. Behind the scenes, they were working tirelessly with our Jehovah's Witness Liaison Committee to get me moved to Englewood hospital that day.

This committee is made up of Jehovah's Witnesses worldwide. Some 1,700 hospital liaison committees form an international network operating in over 110 countries. They are made up of community-based ministers who are Jehovah's Witnesses, who knowledgeably interact with physicians and hospital personnel, social workers, and members of the judiciary. Upon request, they offer the following services, without charge:

o   Provide clinical papers and information from peer-reviewed and respected medical journals on clinical strategies for managing patients without allogeneic blood transfusion.
o   Facilitate physician-to-physician consultations with qualified specialists. Assist with patient transfer when necessary.
o   Clarify ethical issues for Witness patients or clinicians related to medical care. Arrange for pastoral care and practical assistance to hospitalized Witness patients. Just to name a few.

I remembered one of the Elders stating that they would be taking me to Englewood even if he will have to bring me on his back. I was touched that they were working so hard. The hold-up was still on the part of CentraState hospital. After the brothers left that Sunday afternoon at about 1 pm as I sat on the side of my hospital bed I was once again overcome by sadness and despair. At that very moment, I held my head low and quietly prayed. In that quiet and simple prayer, I told Jehovah God that I loved life and wanted to live. I told him that I did not want to die. However, I added that if he felt that my work here on earth was done then I would accept his will. However, I was determined to keep my integrity.

I had barely opened my eyes when the head physician of hematology at CentraState hospital came in to see me. Never had I known of a MD who was so candid, but I give all credit to God. He told me that he knew of my beliefs of not taking blood transfusions, and he honored that. Then he added, "We here at CentraState do not know how to treat patients who do not take blood. If you stay here, you will only end up on a ventilator, but you know where you can go for bloodless medicine?" Where I asked quietly. "Englewood hospital," he stated.

"Well that is where I am trying to go." I cried, but they think I am too ill to travel.

"I will sign the transfer forms for you now releasing you to go to Englewood hospital."

I could not believe my ears. He signed the papers, and I called the Elders from my Congregation and told them. They in turn contacted Englewood who stated that they did not have a bed yet, but they would work on it. Within an hour, a hospital bed had become available; and just like that, Sunday evening January 01, 2012 at 5:00 p.m., I pulled out of CentraState hospital in an ambulance under the care of two nurses. One was in the back with me while I was kept on oxygen and heart monitor. While the other was driving. We arrived at Englewood Hospital at exactly 6:00 p.m. Bypassing the ER, they took me straight to the ICU/CCU unit.

Once I arrived on the unit, oh, what a difference a hospital that treats with bloodless medicine makes. They were ready for me. At the head of my bed was a sign with a big sign "No Blood." Once they got me comfortable in bed, the different physicians assigned to my team, each came in and told me how they were going to care for me during my stay there.

Then a very kind nurse came in to me. She told me she was going to have to stick me to get an IV line so that she could start a bag of iron with normal saline solution. Shortly after there it was, a giant bag of IV Iron with a bag of normal saline of the same size running simultaneously.

"Aww!!" This time my veins did not burn from receiving Iron. Giving IV alone can eat up the best of veins. At that very moment, I felt like a weight had lifted off me, and I knew that I was going to be well taken care of here going forward.

I spent a total of nine days in the ICU/CCU unit at Englewood hospital, and although it was not easy, they were able to save my life. I would like to take the opportunity at this time to thank all those who took very good care of me in my darkest hour including the wonderful and entire Clinical Team at Englewood hospital in Englewood New Jersey. On January 09, 2012, I was able to go home. It was a difficult road ahead, but yes, I was alive. I was home recuperating for another two months and did not return to work until the first week in March 2012. I was able to slowly get back to resume my duties as a continuous care nurse. I guess my work on earth was not done yet. I am glad that my life was spared. Had I not lived, I would not have had the opportunity to meet this incredible human being that I cared for and am about to introduce you to in the next chapter.

Chapter 11

Caring for a Female Legend

As my journey continued, and my body continued to heal, I went on to care for several precious souls throughout the year. Then on October 12, 2012, my next assignment brought me to an assisted living facility that is located in Hamilton in the South Western part of the State.

Here lived LD. She had started her end of life journey. She had an apartment here at the assisted living, and when I arrived, the facility's nurse and aides were present at her bedside. I could see that she was well loved, respected, and was a legend in her own right. As always as is routine for hospice, I completed my assessment on her, rendered p.m. care, medicated, and tucked her in. I must say, she was one of the most beautiful women that I had ever seen. She was ninety years old, but her beautiful form was still intact with the thickest eyebrows and the longest eyelashes one ever did see. Her eyes were striking and just followed you around the room. Although she no longer spoke because of her advanced dementia, make no mistake this woman had left a mark on Society.

Once she was comfortable, I took up my position at a small table close to a corner in her tiny apartment not too far from her bedside. The staff was eager to tell me who she was and how well she was loved. This is because LD was a woman of many talents and interests. As a young woman, she was a stunt car driver and was known as LD. She enjoyed baking, cooking, and sewing. She was especially fond of gardening and feeding the squirrels that lived in her yard. Born in Trenton, LD was a longtime Hamilton area resident. However, by all reports, she was an exceptional woman for her time and even down to our day. She was the only stunt person I had met much less a stuntwoman from the 1950s.

She was New Jersey's first stuntwoman car driver. "She would perform stunt driving using cars in her *Auto Daredevil Thrill Show*. She would often perform her shows at the *Trenton Fairgrounds*. It was similar to the *Joie Chit Wood Hell Driver* shows. They performed stunts on the front straight away of the track. It was precision driving in the truest sense. They did the steeplechase, where four cars, two-by-two, and within inches of each other jumped two ramps, criss-crossed, and jumped two additional ramps, while keeping in perfect formation. The cars are 1951–52 Kaiser Henry Js. They performed the T-bone crash, jumping a ramp, and broadsiding a parked car, flipping both cars into a T. They may also have performed a ramp-to-ramp jump: one car over and one car under. Very exciting stuff." Wow are you dizzy yet! This I read directly from a newspaper article archive that was posted in her room.

What an amazing woman. This was a woman who was also a mother to a son and daughter; and of course, she was a wife. Her husband RD, who at this time had predeceased her, was also a stunt driver; however, it was LD who was the star even for her time. She was a loving mother, grandmother, and great grandmother. Her family by this time had arrived to visit her. Her daughter is also a well-known Hollywood movie producer and was going to be flying in later to see her hopefully.

The family came and left, and I continued to remain at LD's bedside that night. She would occasionally open her eyes as she continued her transition. She had all the signs and symptoms of active death and dying, which was evident by mottling to both legs, labored breathing, and gurgling. Quite naturally, I stayed on top of making sure that she received all the medications that she needed for each symptom that she would have. Soon she was very comfortable. I also used the aromatherapy essence of the journey that is customized for patients with end stage dementia. This really caused her to get to a place where her body became very relaxed. She completed her journey at 1:00 a.m. on October 13, 2012. I was there with her, and the nurses and aides from the facility all came in to bid their beloved town and resident legend, LD, goodbye.

I notified her family, and they did not want to return since they had visited earlier. Her daughter did not get to come in to see her at the facility, but one thing was for sure, her plan was to see her at the funeral home once she arrived in New Jersey several hours later. She was pronounced, and once the funeral directors came, my usual ritual walk to the hearse waiting outside meant so much more. There was no family waiting back in her apartment, so when I came back inside, I made sure that I locked up her apartment and handed over the key to the nurse on duty.

I walked away that early morning and could not believe how life and circumstances had brought me in the presence of someone who was a part of New Jersey's rich history. Note to self, the State of New Jersey has produced a lot of legends, some have unfortunately passed on, but others are very much alive.

Kudos to the Great State of New Jersey.

CHAPTER 12

An Assignment that Lasted for Only a Few Hours but Left a Lifetime of Memory

A few months later, on March 17, 2013, my work experience brought me up close and personal with another individual that caused me to be placed in direct contact with a piece of American dynasty. Allow me please to tell you how this unfolded.

First, let me give you a look at the background of this unique lady. She was a nurse, so I was determined to go the extra mile to make sure that she was going to be very comfortable. Her name was CK, and she was from the county of Burlington. Burlington county is also at the South Western part of the state about thirty minutes south of Hamilton Township. She lived at an Assisted Living facility in Burlington Township, and she was eighty-nine years old.

With a soul, character, spirit, and voice full of beauty, kindness, and love, she was described to me by the nursing staff and family as the most wonderful mother, grandmother, wife, sister, aunt, mother-in-law, and friend. Her sense of humor, laughter, and loving spirit is fondly remembered. Nothing made her happier they say than being surrounded by her family, with a dog by her side, treasuring all the times of just being together.

She was a school nurse at Burlington City elementary schools, member of the Burlington County School Nurses Association, RN volunteer for the American Red Cross, and member of Young at Heart's Club.

CK served as an ensign in the U.S. Navy Nurse Corps where she met and married LK, a Navy pilot and the love of her life. Known as the "songbird" in high school, she was a gifted singer who lit up a room when she entered, greeting everyone with a song and always a smile. *What a talented woman*, I thought.

Her greatest passion in life was raising her seven children and being a wonderful grandmother to her three beloved grandsons. Running a close third was her love of ice cream. She was also an avid golfer, loved to play the piano, and thoroughly enjoyed many days at the beach with her family.

Her deep devotion and love of the Lord, which radiated from her heart and touched many lives, was the true essence of who CK was. She had a special gift of helping people with her words and her compassion. CK stayed on this Earth just long enough to celebrate her 89th birthday, not wanting to miss a party and hear her family's laughter one last time.

How do you top that? I thought. I don't need to. My job was to render the best care that I possibly could to this remarkable lady as the final curtain closes on her life. I was told by her primary nurse at the facility that her family was on their way.

She also told me that they were coming from different areas. Some were coming from New Jersey, but one daughter would be coming from Massachusetts. The nurse also added that she was the family member of a VIP. I thought to myself that all the patients I cared for are VIPs. I have an even softer spot for patients who were nurses because I know how much they have to deal with while working as a nurse. Nonetheless, that word VIP lingered in the back of my mind. I was curious for the reveal but the staff nurse would not share anymore details.

I went to her room at 7:00 pm, and there she was, all but ninety pounds due to her being stricken with Alzheimer's disease. One look at her, and it's clear for me to see that she was on the final hours of her journey. She was not opening her eyes, was unresponsive to touch and she had Cheyne-Stokes breathing.

Cheyne breathing is a pattern of interrupted breathing called Cheyne-Stokes breathing, and for some, there may be noisy breathing sometimes, called the death rattle. Cheyne-Stokes breathing is a pattern of breathing often present in a dying patient. The person takes several breaths followed by a pause in breathing of several seconds. She was comfortable though in spite of her breathing. Prior to my arrival, the staff nurse had medicated her with Morphine. I assessed her, checked that her oxygen was in place; and cleaned her up so that she was clean, fresh, and dry and comfortable.

She never opened her eyes, but I whispered in her ears to hang in there since her family was on the way. I tried to keep her from slipping away by telling her what the weather was like outside. Although I knew that she could not answer me, I was trying to keep her going as it were until her family arrived.

Soon, six of her seven children arrived, and they all said their goodbyes. I provided emotional support to them and conversed and answered all questions and concerns that they had. I soon realized that her daughter from Massachusetts had to be the VIP. I wondered who she was, but I was too afraid to ask her siblings who were present.

An hour later, in walked her daughter AEK—a tall, elegant, and well-composed woman. I did not recognize her either. When her husband JK emerged shortly after then, I knew exactly why the nurse had told me that she was related to a VIP. I recognized JK from the Commercials that he does on TV and knew that he was related to a very prominent and powerful American political family. Truly a member of an American dynasty.

AEK and JK were very humble and thankful for all the care that I was giving their mom and mother-in-law. I have to say, they were two of the most down-to-earth people I have ever met. They both hugged me over, and over while they thanked me profusely. They too went to her bedside to say their final goodbyes.

I offered to leave the room to give them privacy, but they wanted me to stay. I soon realized that AEK was a woman of faith. She wanted to reward me, but I told her that I could not accept a gift per say. It was against company policy. She was disappointed. Not to be deterred, she pulled out a card that qouted Psalms 130, which stated count on God. I have to tell you, it has been almost five years now; but unto this day, I still keep that card at the head of my bed.

Whenever I am troubled by anything, I just take a look at it; and it soothes my heart, mind, and soul. I have to say that this little card with the Psalms far outweighs any material gift that I could have been given. The material thing I am sure would have long perished. AEK and her husband chatted with her large loving extended family then bid all goodbye, hopped into their waiting limousine and headed back to Massachusetts. The rest of her siblings also left, and once again, I was alone with CK. It was 11:00 p.m. by the time all her family left.

CK was really "traveling." Her periods of apnea were getting longer and longer. I sat real close to her bed. There was no need for synthetic medications at this time. She was very comfortable. I think she was waiting for all her children to come. I held her hands and gently stroked her face while I thanked her for serving as a nurse in the different organizations. At 11:30 p.m., CK left this earth. I went out to the nurse's station and informed the staff nurse, together we notified her children who had left earlier. They took it well. All were at peace including AEK. That little card that occupies a small space in the headboard of my bed is a constant reminder of the day I took care of CK that allowed me to meet her large and loving family and allowed me to meet the offspring of one of America's most powerful families to date.

CHAPTER 13

The Final Exit

If you are familiar with New Jersey by now, you would have come to know that everyone lives off an exit on the Garden State Parkway.

The outside world does not understand the rich complexity of that statement. They associate it with the area directly around the Meadowlands and outside of New York without fully appreciating the intricacies. Your exit number off the parkway actually gives the person talking to you a good sense of what kind of New Jerseyan you are. That is are you from North, Central or South Jersey. If you do not actually live off an exit on the parkway, you live off an exit of the New Jersey Turnpike.

My last continuous care case was in the town of Eatontown 105 exit off the Garden State Parkway in Central New Jersey on June **14**, 2016. This was at the home of fifty eight year old registered nurse, wife, and mother, BB. BB had been a resident of Eatontown for thirty years. She was a registered nurse at a prominent nursing home, located in Neptune, New Jersey. Her loving husband JB, beloved son BB, and daughter-in-law LB, all related that she had a passion and love for animal rescue and was the founding member of Tails of Hope, an all-breed, nonprofit, no-kill 5O1C3 Animal Rescue organization serving New Jersey.

She was an avid runner, a member of the Jersey Shore Running Club, and participated in marathons they held. She loved traveling, the beach, and most of all, spending time with her family. Her family was the great love of her life as well as her many friends she made over the years. Unfortunately, this lady—who was beautiful inside and out—had been battling brain cancer for several years, and now she was losing the battle.

I was sent to care for her, but this time though, I was on the day shift and not the night shift. I got off exit 105 off the Garden State Parkway and arrived at her home at 8:00 a.m. that morning. I was the first continuous care nurse to visit and so I was opening the case. She had come unto service the day before, and last night, she reportedly seized for about one hour straight. These seizures were tonic-clonic seizures, which were formerly known as grand mal seizures. The hospice on call Nurse was called out and had medicated her with Neurontin which finally gave her some relief.

When I arrived, she was in a deep sleep on a sofa in her living room upstairs. Her concerned husband, JB, was very worried about her and reported that it was the first time for the past sixteen years since she has been battling brain cancer that she had seized for so long. The length and violence that came with the seizure proved to be too much for her body, and it had wiped her out.

Soon her only child and son, BB, and his wife who were staying over came out to meet me; and both related the same story about the length of the seizure. BB also added that she was actually blind and had lost the use of the left side after seizures last night. Only yesterday during the day, they reported when she was being signed unto hospice, she was actually walking around.

For the past sixteen years, she had been travelling back and forth to Memorial Sloane and Kettering Hospital. She has had multiple brain surgeries, the family reported including a craniotomy. This last visit a week ago, as is the case with many of these cases after a time, there was nothing more that they could do. She had to be placed on hospice.

In spite of her grave prognosis, the family was not expecting her to decline this rapidly. They were very heart broken. As I assessed her, I realized that she was not waking up. She was breathing easily and unlabored, but her eyes were tightly close. When I checked her eyes with my flashlight, the pupils were fixed and nonreactive to light.

The usual routine ensued of cleaning her up to get her ready for the day.

She was unable to swallow her medications at this point. So I reached out to the RN case manager to help have MD change her medication to Ativan gel and to have it delivered as soon as possible so that I could give it. She was very comfortable lying on the couch, and I hated to have to move her, but our DME company had just delivered her hospital bed and oxygen and had set it all up. I knew that I could not allow her to stay on the couch. Her room was set up one floor down so this was going to be a behemoth of a task to transfer her since she was not able to bear any weight. I enlisted the help of her son, Daughter-in-law, and husband to execute the move.

We finally got her comfortable in the hospital bed with low air loss mattress. Since the cancer had reduced her to a mere seventy pounds I wanted to make sure that she was comfortable and that her skin would not break down on the bony prominence areas. I quickly applied oxygen set at two liters per minute as was ordered by the physician. All through the move from her living room upstairs, to all four of us carrying her downstairs and then transferring her to the bed, she never moved and never woke up. I then knew that she too had started her end of life journey.

Sure she was still breathing easy and unlabored, but she was not waking up. This is one of the fastest decline I had ever seen. In less than forty-eight hours, she went from alert and oriented to person, place, and time to being unresponsive to verbal and tactile stimuli. It was a devastating blow to the family, and they wept openly. The entire hospice team was brought on board which included the RN case manager who handles the case and the hospice social worker and chaplain to comfort them.

They were very grateful for the emotional and spiritual support, as well as the nursing care that she was receiving. She had a very big extended family which included her eighty-four-year-old mother, sisters, brother, and countless in laws, nieces, and nephews just to name a few. I got her ready for the day and repositioned her so that her limbs could be out stretched. I placed pillows under and behind her to foster extra comfort.

She looked very relaxed, and I was glad about this since it brought some comfort to the family. I kept her medicated with Ativan gel to prevent her from seizing again, with Morphine to ensure that she would remain free from pain and air hunger, and Levsin tablets for her increased secretions since she had started to have secretions settling in her throat. These throat secretions are what later become the well-known death rattle, which is normally heard shortly before a patient pass away.

I was instructed by my nursing office that I should stay until 8:00 p.m. that night. BB needed to be medicated every three hours, and her family was too distraught to give it, so an LPN nurse had to be present at all times. Several visitors came throughout the day once the family texted them with the news that she was now comatose.

As I had mentioned at the outset, BB was very active in her community. So many people from different walks-of-life were among the visitors that day. She was the doppelganger of Kate Jackson from the 1970s TV show Charlie's Angels. Her pictures before she got sick were absolutely beautiful. She was just a shell of her former self now, yet her family and friends told the story of her true beauty which lay inside. She was a nurse and was kind and compassionate to both humans and animals.

As my shift came to a close at 8:00 p.m. that night, I left her comfortable in the care of the incoming nurse. I was happy that I had left her in the care of this nurse. She is a very kind, compassionate, and thorough nurse. BB deserved the best, and I knew she would take very good care of her.

Yet I was concerned. Why you may ask? Well BB was only fifty-eight years old and so could not get Medicare insurance because she was so young. The law of the land does not allow Medicare benefits until you are sixty-five years old or older. She had private insurance, and our RN case manager had told me that we probably would not be able to continue providing continuous care for only but two more days because that is all that her insurance will pay for. I thought to myself who is going to take care of her.

The next day I arrived at 8:00 a.m., and I could see that BB had declined rapidly. She was holding on though. The outgoing hospice nurse had left her nice and clean, and she was comfortable; and there was no evidence of pain or air hunger. Her family was sitting vigil at her bedside. Her husband asked me to step outside for a minute because he wanted to speak with me. Once we were out in the living room area, he started to cry and asked me how much longer I think his beloved wife would last. I told him I honestly did not know but think that the journey would soon come to an end. You see, he too was aware that their insurance was not going to pay for her continuous care nursing much longer. He did not have the money to pay for private nursing care in the home, and they did not qualify for Medicaid, so that she could go to a facility to stay since they had assets.

He was in such a bind, he thought. I gave him reassurance and told him that I would try to help. I discussed his concerns with the RN case manager when she came for her RN visit at 10:00 a.m. that morning and told her that we have to help BB. I told her that as nurses, we needed to stand by her. I felt that if we left her without nursing care, it would be like leaving a fellow soldier on the battle-field. She reassured me that she would discuss this with the powers that be in our company to see what we could do to help as nurses.

After giving the RN case manager a detailed report on BB's present condition, I went back inside her room to continue to sit vigil at her bedside. She still had not awaken from her unresponsive state, yet she was resting comfortably and was at peace. At 2:00 p.m. that day, I received a call from the RN case manager that since she was comfortable and was now asymptomatic for seizures, pain, and increased secretions, we could not continue with continuous care as per her insurance guidelines. Continuous care would have to end with my shift that night at 7:00 p.m. It was a crushing defeat, and I did not know how I was going to deliver this news to the family.

I really felt that we were letting a fellow soldier and colleague down although I understood that her insurance laws had to be followed.

To be quite honest, I did not know how I was going to face the family with this news. Soon, a thought came to me as I sat staring at her as she lay helplessly in her bed. I knew that I could not leave her. So I reached out to my clinical director and told her that I would stay until 12:00 a.m. which would be five hours later than my scheduled time just to make sure that she was comfortable and that the family could get some rest. This way although difficult, they would be up with her from 12:00 a.m. until 8:00 a.m. when the RN case manager would return for a visit.

When I broke the news finally to her husband, son, and daughter-in-law, they were grateful that I was staying but very sad and worried that they would not be having nursing care. I validated their feelings and reassured them that I would teach LB her daughter-in-law how to change and clean her during the night should she be soiled. This I did, and LB was a natural. I told her think of her mother-in-law who although she was an adult because of the illness she had reverted to the baby stages of life.

I also taught LB how to administer the necessary medications that she would need throughout the night. She was a quick study and was able to return demonstration. When I left that night at midnight, I knew that LB would take care of BB; but I knew that if she lasted for another week or so, it would be very difficult for the family since they were up during the day too.

That night, once I was home, I kept wondering how else could I help her. The next morning, I woke up expecting to go to another assignment when I received a call from my nursing office instructing me to go back to BB for a twelve-hour shift. Our administration had made the decision to not bill for continuous care but to eat the cost of keeping a nurse at the bedside.

They wanted to see her through until the end as a fellow nurse sister. We did not want to leave her to take her journey alone. Her family could not believe the generosity of the company. They were ever so grateful, and I continued to render loving care with all my heart to this well-deserved and precious human being. I provided care to her for the next week during the day until she passed away peacefully on the afternoon of Wednesday, June 22, 2016, with her loving family by her side along with the entire hospice team including, the social worker, bereavement coordinator, and chaplain, and myself.

Although grieving her loss, her family expressed that their hearts were brimming with joy because I along with the clinical team had gone above and beyond for their beloved BB. I was glad I could help in my own small way. I would have done it again for her or any one in need like that a thousand times over. Why? Because it was the right thing to do. She had given of herself as a nurse so many times. How could we leave her on the battlefield? I just could not.

So on June 22, 2016, after I provided post mortem care to BB and saw her taken into the care of the funeral directors, I did my final walk to the hearse with her. By this time, her large extended family had arrived; and they needed time to grieve and comfort each other, so I bid them a final goodbye amidst hugs, tears, and extreme gratitude from all.

Soon I entered exit 105 for the last time and got off at exit 100 and headed for my home. My work in continuous care was officially over. I had been offered a new position in the Company's intake department as of July 5, 2016. I have been there over a year now and no longer regularly do continuous care. I reached a milestone in my life earlier this year when I turned fifty, yet I have no regrets. It is often said, "No greater gift can a human give another than to take care of them knowing that they can never repay you." It has been an interesting trip serving as a continuous care nurse, and I cherish all the experiences and all my patients and their families that I have met along the way. Yes, they will live on in my memory until I too take my final journey.

ABOUT THE AUTHOR

My precious friend, Trudy,
gone but never forgotten

Elizabeth Walters is a hospice nurse with over fourteen years of hands-on hospice experience taking care of terminally ill patients. She currently works as nurse intake coordinator with a large and prestigious hospice agency, in New Jersey. She lives with her family in the northeast.

CPSIA information can be obtained
at www.ICGtesting.com
Printed in the USA
BVHW021254041022
648621BV00018B/1335

9 781643 502120